Come on a wild journey as you learn your Victorian Modern Cursive script.

My name is

My school is

Learning goal: *To improve knowledge of the alphabet in Victorian Modern Cursive script*

Success criteria:

- *I can trace and write all lower-case and capital letters of the alphabet in Victorian Modern Cursive.*
- *I can trace and write all lower-case and capital letters of the alphabet in Victorian Modern Cursive using appropriate size, spacing and slope.*

Are you ready to write?

Posture

Is your back resting against the chair?

Are your feet flat on the floor?

Paper position

left-handed

Are you holding the paper steady with your non-writing hand?

right-handed

Pencil grip

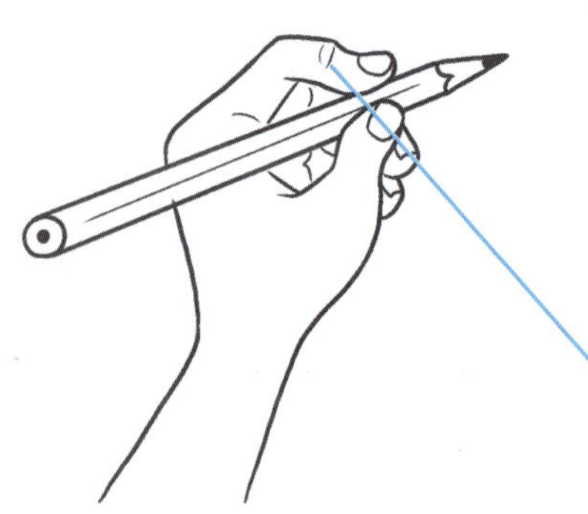

Is there only one finger on top of your pen or pencil?

Left-handers, hold your pen or pencil a little higher so you can see your handwriting!

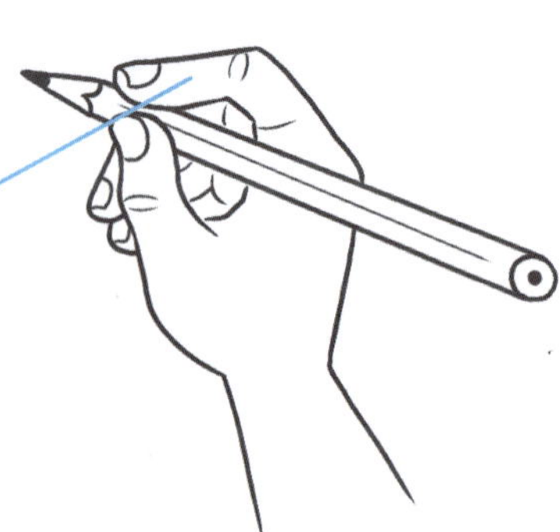

1, 2, 3, 4! Are my feet flat on the floor?
5, 6, 7, 8! Is my back up nice and straight?
9, 10, 11, 12! Show me how your pencil's held!
Thumb and pointer side-by-side, lucky tall one takes a ride!

ISBN: 9780170424059

Unjoined letters

Revise your lower-case and capital letters.

aA bB cC dD eE fF gG

hH iI jJ kK lL mM nN

oO pP qQ rR sS tT uU

vV wW xX yY zZ

Copy the text.

This is the Victorian Infant

Cursive handwriting script.

Write these words in all capital letters.

Lower-case letters	Capital letters
australia	
indonesia	
spain	
botswana	
canada	

Place a tick above the words that should start with a capital letter. Write only those words on the lines below.

april few monday city

melbourne most harry

english elephant she's i'm

Heads, bodies and tails

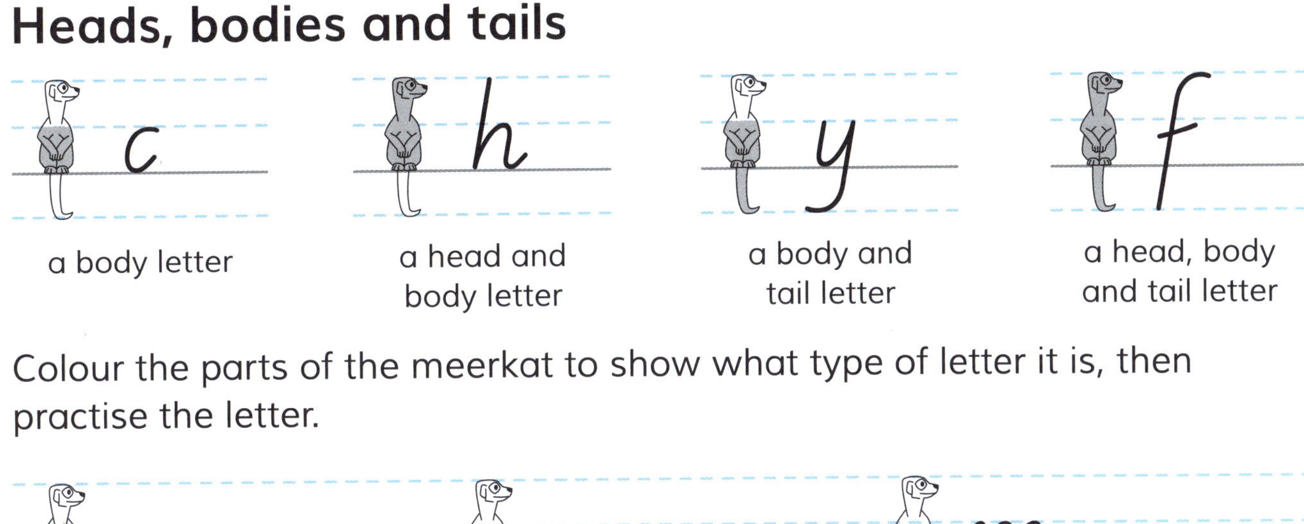

Colour the parts of the meerkat to show what type of letter it is, then practise the letter.

Can you group the lower-case letters of the alphabet? Complete the rows.

Body letters (13)

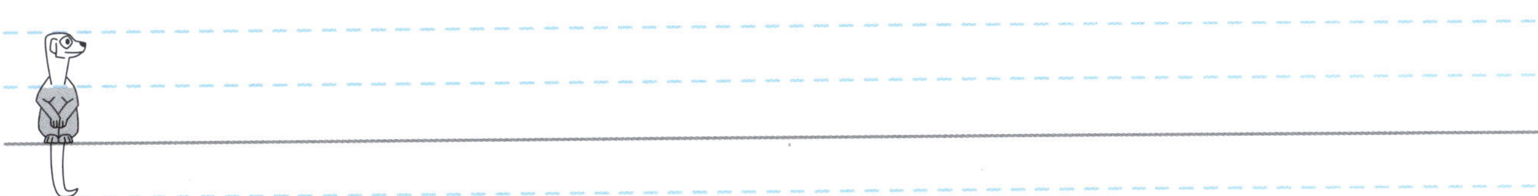

Head and body letters (6)

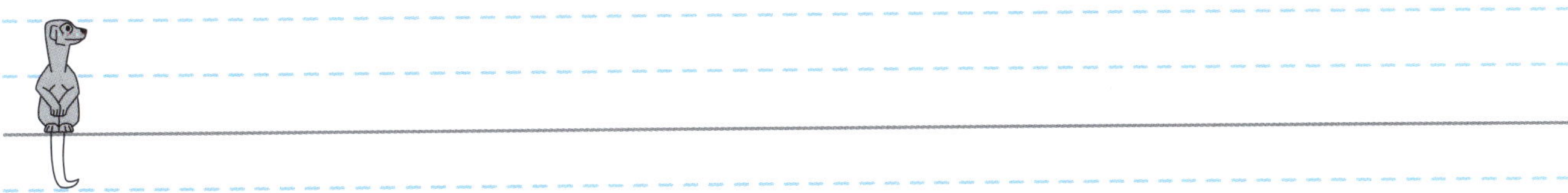

Body and tail letters (6)

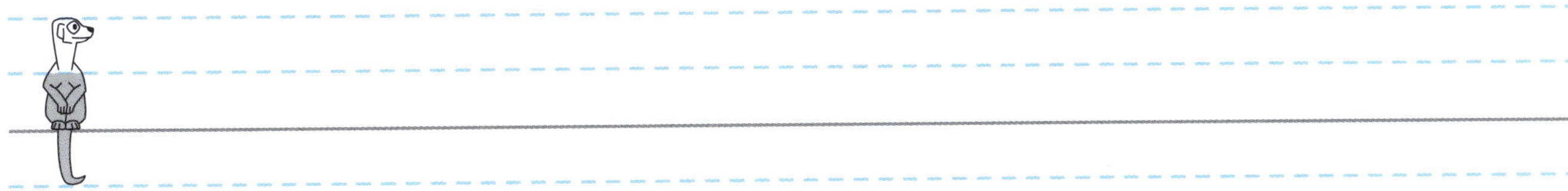

Head, body and tail letter (1)

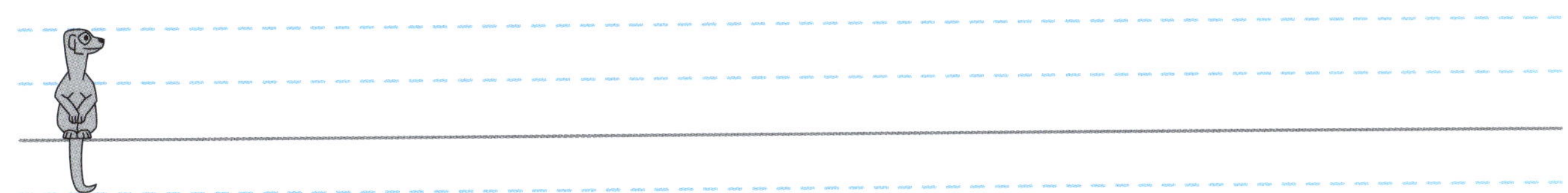

Patterning exercises

Trace and copy these patterns.

Letter groups

Write the letters belonging to each letter group.
Write the letters in the order they appear in the alphabet.

Downstroke letters (4)

i

Closed anti-clockwise letters (5)

a

Open anti-clockwise letters (9)

b

Clockwise letters (8)

h

Read the the following sentence, then:

- Underline the downstroke letters.
- Place a dot above the closed anti-clockwise letters.
- Place a tick above the open anti-clockwise letters.
- Circle the clockwise letters.

Bar-tailed godwits
migrate from Alaska to
New Zealand every year.

Downstroke letters

Trace the downstroke letters. Complete the row.

l i t j

Copy these words beginning with downstroke letters.

leap lion lizard lemur

idea important isn't insect

tallest teeth turtle toucan

jumped jaguar jellyfish

Write some words of your own beginning with downstroke letters.

Closed anti-clockwise letters

These letters all start near the magic line and move in an anti-clockwise direction.

Trace the closed anti-clockwise letters.

a d g q o

magic line

Copy these words beginning with closed anti-clockwise letters.

again attack alligator

dolphin distance dingo

giraffe giant gorilla gecko

quickly quiet quokka quoll

often over octopus orca

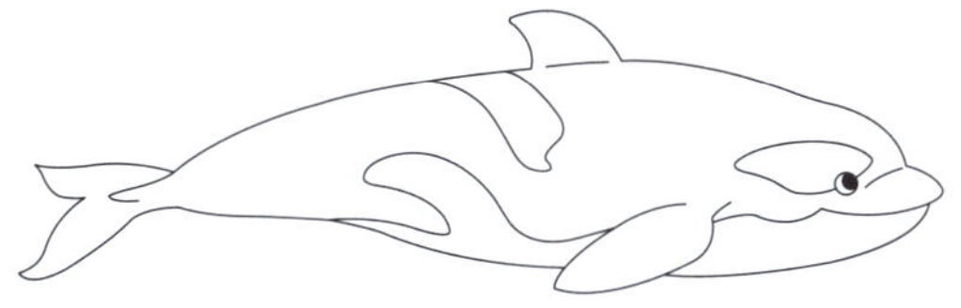

Open anti-clockwise letters

Add the letters in the open anti-clockwise letter group to the alphabet below.

a __ __ d __ __ g h i j k l m n

o p q r __ t __ __ __ x __ z

Copy the sentences below. Then place a tick above all the words beginning with an open anti-clockwise letter.

In the valley of the extinct

volcano, emus wander,

wombats dig underground

and a young sparrow calls

to its father from its nest.

Clockwise letters

Trace and copy the clockwise letters.

These letters move in a clockwise direction.

n m p r h k x z

Copy the sentences below. Then place a tick above all the words beginning with a clockwise letter.

Lions roar loudly to protect

their prides. A male kudu

can have huge horns.

A herd of zebras can be

prey for hungry hyenas.

Parts of letters

Trace the words in the box, then add them to the diagram below.

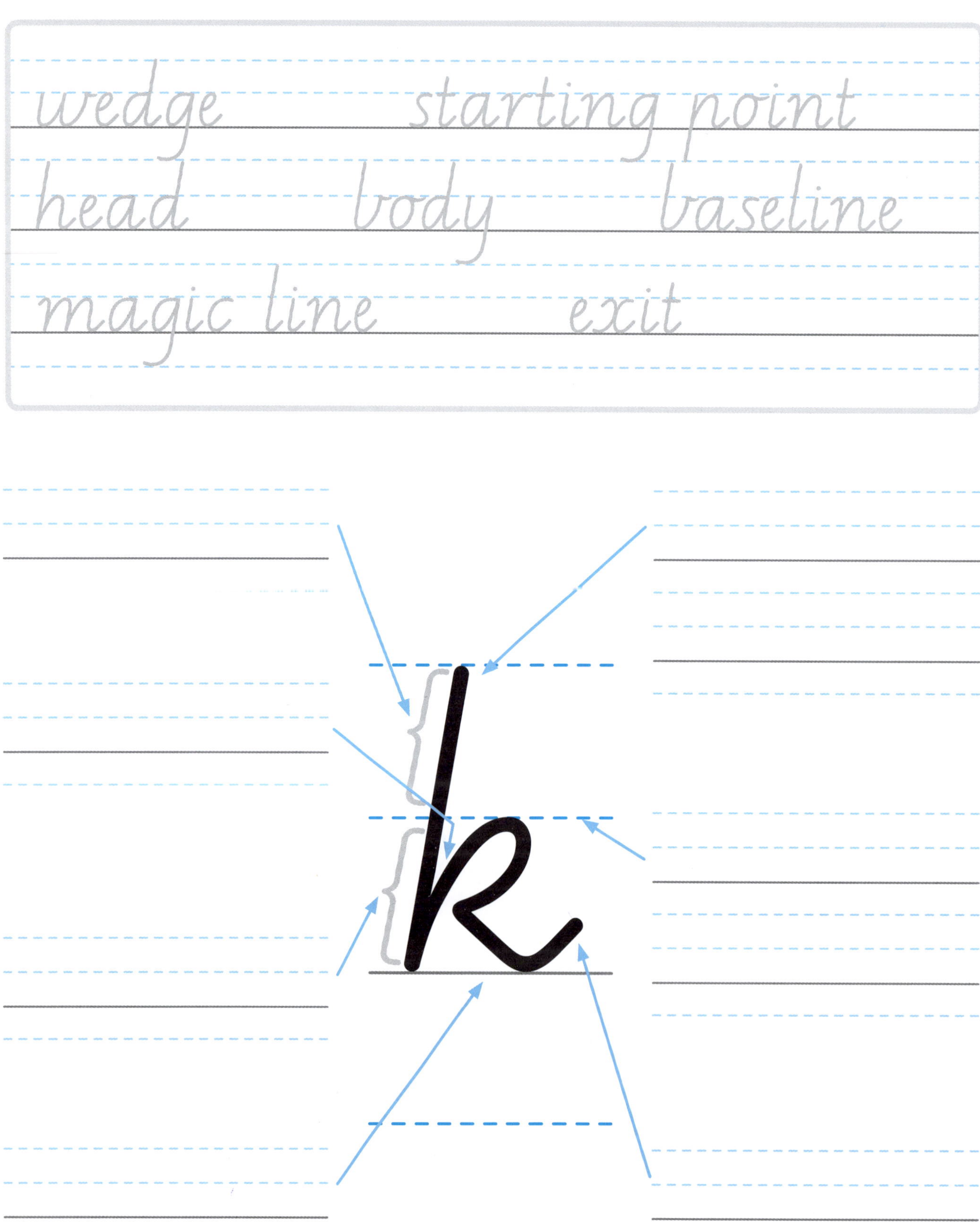

Draw a dot to show the starting point of each letter, then practise the letter. Complete the line.

d

f

b

h

p

o

x

e

a

w

Colour all the wedges in the sentence.

Monarch butterflies migrate to warmer places in winter.

get.ga/PMWA160

ISBN: 9780170424059

An exit flick is a way out of a letter. It helps you join to the next letter.

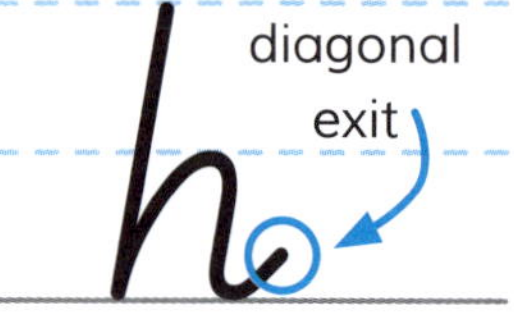

Some letters have diagonal exits. These exits are near the baseline, or the bottom of the letter.

Trace the letters with diagonal exits, then circle the exits.

a c d e h i k

l m n p t u x

Copy these words to practise your diagonal exits.

albatross crocodile dolphin

hyena insect kingfisher

foxes meerkat numbat

Some letters have horizontal exits. These exits are near the magic line.

Trace the letters with horizontal exits, then circle the exits.

b o r v w

Copy these words to practise your horizontal exits.

raccoon vulture wombat

n

A rounded entry is a way into a letter. It helps you join to the letter.

Trace the letters with rounded entries, then circle the entries.

m n r x z

Copy these words to practise your rounded entries.

rhinoceros lynx lizard

ISBN: 9780170424059

Can you group the lower-case letters with exits and entries?

Exits only (15)

Rounded entries (5)

Exits and entries (3)

Some exits and entries are missing from the words below. Rewrite the words, adding the exits and entries correctly.

parrot jellyfish crocodile

bat monkey seal turtle nest

Self-assessment: Unjoined letters

Copy the text.

Colour is important to
butterflies. It helps them to
hide from their enemies.
The patterns on the wings of
a butterfly are symmetrical.

Self-assessment

Rate your unjoined letters.

☐ I need more practice.

☐ They're fairly good.

☐ They look great!

ISBN: 9780170424059

Introducing joins

giraffe **unjoined**

giraffe **cursive**

In cursive, most letters are joined.

Join lines join one letter to the next. They should be fast and direct.

Try adding a join line to each letter pair.

ci eu av ti

dn hi ki lu

mu ni ty cu

Diagonal joins

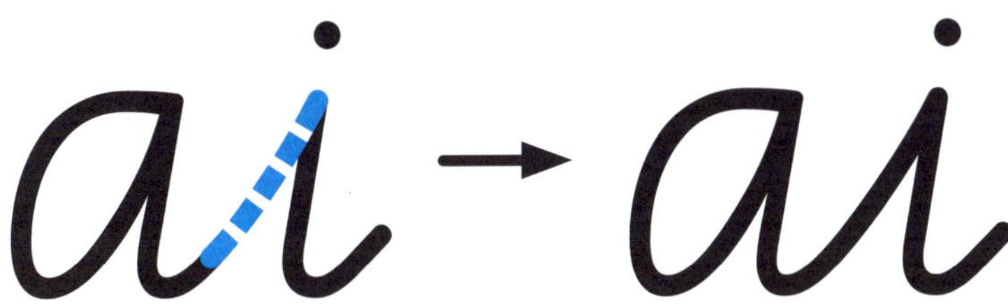

Extend the diagonal exit of the first letter high to join to the next letter.

Most letters meet at the magic line.

Trace and copy these letter pairs with diagonal joins.

ai ap au av aw ay am

an ar ci cu cy cr di do

du dy dr ei ep eu ew

ey em en er ex hi hu

ISBN: 9780170424059

Trace and copy these letter pairs with diagonal joins.

iw im in iz ky li lo lp

lu ly mi mm mn mp mu

my ni nn pi pu py ti

tr tu ty ue ui um un

ur ue ux xy xi xy xi

Trace and copy these words using diagonal joins.

air jaw monkey stingray

Copy the alphabet with diagonal joins.

abcdefghijklmnopqrstuvwxyz

Copy these words with diagonal joins.

time her like cheetah

then they them tell

quite put little link

bee pile nine marlin

ISBN: 9780170424059

Diagonal joins to head and body letters

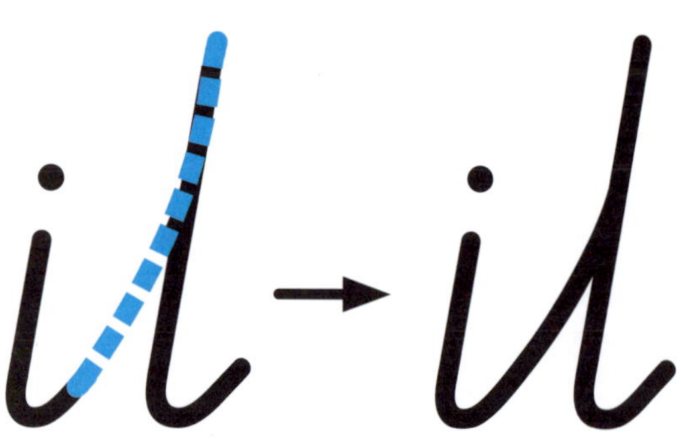

When joining to head and body letters, sweep up to the top and down again.

Trace and copy these letter pairs with diagonal joins to head and body letters.

eb el et ib il it lb lt

mb nt th tt ub ul ut

Choose a letter pair from above to make a word on each line below.

b _____ fa _____ h _____

l _____ pa _____ n _____

co _____ gr _____ ro _____

Copy these words with diagonal joins to head and body letters.

about invitation chameleon

spill buckle almost channel

lantern goat cheetah nestle

Here is a wild animal joke for you.

Trace and copy.

Q: What is the biggest ant in the world?

A: An eleph-ant.

ISBN: 9780170424059

Complete the line, practising the diagonal join.

ly ly

Rewrite the word, using any diagonal joins and adding -ly.

careful + ly → carefully

quiet + ly →

quick + ly →

loud + ly →

soft + ly →

Complete the line, practising the diagonal join.

er er

Rewrite the word, using any diagonal joins and adding -er.

long + er →

strong + er →

loud + er →

fast + er →

Add -ly or -er to these words. Make sure your new words are spelt correctly.

bright →

deep →

weak →

keen →

slow →

part →

poor →

thick →

tall →

short →

smart →

swift →

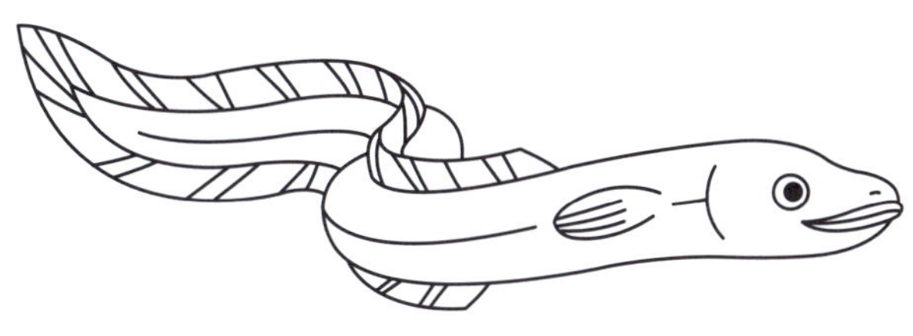

ISBN: 9780170424059

Practising diagonal joins to 'e'

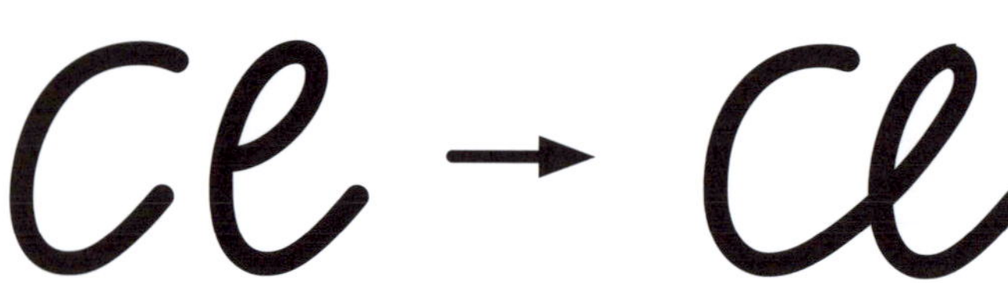

When joining diagonally to 'e', change the shape of the 'e' slightly.

Trace and copy these letter pairs.

ae ce de he ie ke

le me ne pe te ue

Copy these words with diagonal joins to 'e'.

blue whale near valley

underwater pen moment

camel faster elephant

ISBN: 9780170424059

Diagonal joins to 'f'

When making a diagonal join to 'f', continue the exit of the letter before and form a loop. Lift your pen or pencil before adding the crossbar.

Trace and copy these letter pairs with diagonal joins to 'f'.

if af lf ef uf mf nf

Copy these words with diagonal joins to 'f'.

life safety wolf horrified

after magnificent peaceful

ISBN: 9780170424059

Diagonal joins to modified 's'

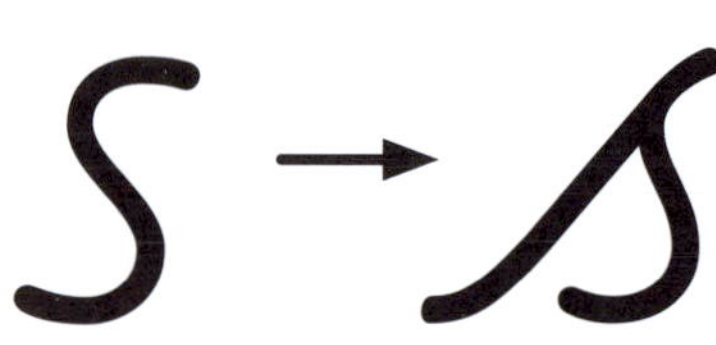

When joining diagonally to the letter 's', you can modify the shape of the 's' so there is less to retrace. This will help you to write faster!

Trace these letter pairs with diagonal joins to 's'.

is as ls es us ms ns

Trace and copy these words with diagonal joins to 's'.

whales oceans pods calves

Practise joining diagonally to 's'. Copy the text.

Dozens of frisky, noisy seals

escaped the ruthless and

fast-moving killer whales.

Diagonal joins from 's'

Joining from the bottom of the letter 's' can speed up your handwriting, because it doesn't require a pencil lift. Retrace along the bottom of the letter.

Trace and copy these letter pairs with diagonal joins from 's'.

se sh si sk sl sm sn

sp sr st su sy sw

get.ga/PMWA161

Copy these words with diagonal joins from 's'.

inside kingfisher island

mouse snail sparrow nest

insect shark understand

ISBN: 9780170424059

Diagonal joins from 'q'

qu

A 'q' can be tricky – you need to change direction and go all the way up to the top.

Don't be quarrelsome! The movement is the same every time – a 'q' is always followed by a 'u'.

Trace and copy.

q q q q q q q q q q

qu qu qu qu qu qu

A quokka looks like a small

kangaroo. Many quokkas

live on Rottnest Island.

Double letter pairs with diagonal joins

ess

When double 's' comes after a diagonal join, make the second 's' look like the first.

tt

When crossing double 't', you can use one crossbar.

Copy these words with double letter pairs.

baleen waterfall jellyfish

millions message address

glass flightless attack see

butterfly attempt better

ISBN: 9780170424059

Self-assessment: Diagonal joins

Copy these letter pairs.

ai il ly er ce af es se qu tt

I hope you like animal jokes!

Rewrite the joke below. Use any joins you already know.

Q: What did the pony say

when it had a sore throat?

A: I'm a little hoarse.

Self-assessment

Rate your diagonal joins.

☐ I need to work on them.

☐ They're getting there.

☐ They look great!

ISBN: 9780170424059

Touch joins

The following letters use an anti-clockwise movement.

a c d g q

When you join to one of these letters, make a long exit from the letter before. Then, lift your pen or pencil and drop in the second letter, touching the exit on the way down.

pencil lift

na

Try these letters with long exits.

n m i e a d

h k t l c

Diagonal joins to anti-clockwise letters can be tricky, so we use touch joins.

ISBN: 9780170424059

Use two colours to trace the touch joins. Make the exit of the first letter longer, and change pencils to drop in the second letter. The arrows show the pencil lifts.

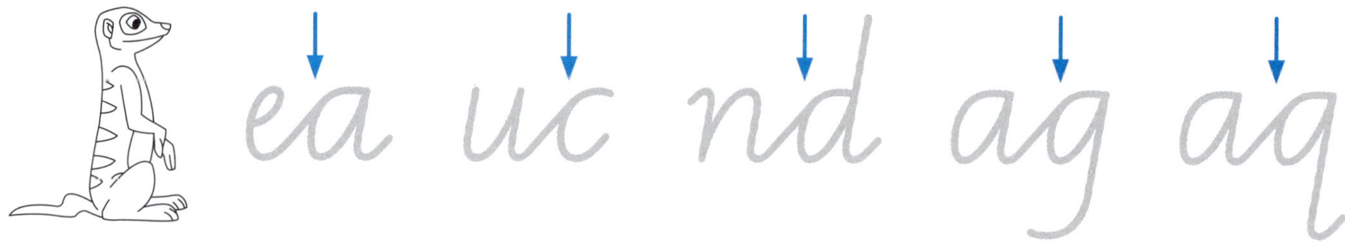

Try some more letter pairs using two different colours. Copy.

na nc nd ng na nc nd

ac ad ag ac ad ag ac

da dd da dd da dd da

ia ic id ig ia ic id

ea ec ed eg eq ea ec

ISBN: 9780170424059

Draw arrows to show the touch joins.

animal predator scales

attack habitat mammal

claws swimming land

get.ga/PMWA162

Practise your touch joins. Copy the text.

The echidna is a mammal that lays eggs. When an egg hatches, a hairless, bean-sized baby, or puggle, is born.

ISBN: 9780170424059

Create a name for this puggle using as many touch joins as possible.

Count the number of touch joins the words below would have in cursive writing. Prove your answers by writing the words in cursive.

squeaked ☐ gliding ☐ puggle ☐

Copy these words with touch joins. Underline every touch join.

echidna guard backpack

edge magnificent suddenly

change caught meadow

aground dance wetlands

ISBN: 9780170424059

Self-assessment: Touch joins

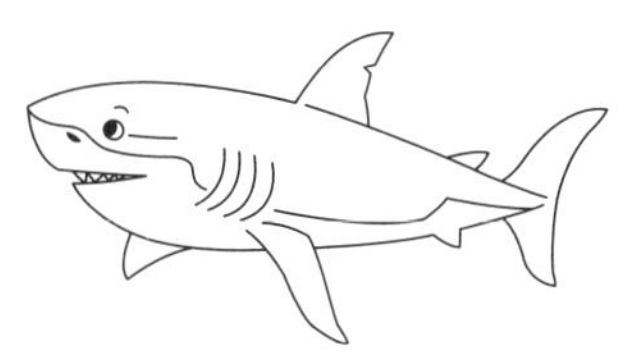

Copy the text.

Blue whales have no teeth.

Baby swans are called cygnets.

Sharks never stop swimming.

Butterflies taste with their feet.

Baby alligators are hatchlings.

Self-assessment

Rate your touch joins.

☐ I need more practice.

☐ They're good.

☐ They're great!

ISBN: 9780170424059

Horizontal joins

The letters that finish near the magic line join horizontally to the next letter.

b o r v w

magic line

Extend the horizontal exit of the first letter right across to meet the next letter at the magic line.

When making a horizontal join, don't dip the join too low.

✓ on ✗ on

Trace and copy.

bi bu br by oi om

on or ou ov ow oy

oz op vi vu vy ri

wombat favourite wrong

ISBN: 9780170424059

Trace and copy.

rm rn rr ru ry rp

wi wn wr wu wy

warm burrow winter

wren brown snowy

brumby dove hopping lion

Write some words of your own with horizontal joins.

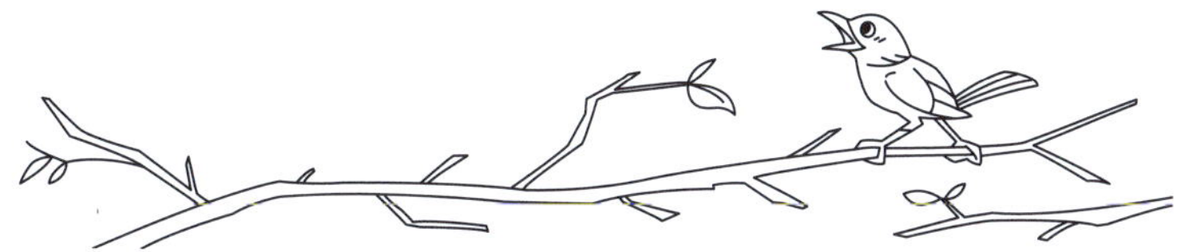

ISBN: 9780170424059

Practising horizontal joins to anti-clockwise letters

When making a horizontal join to a, c, d, g, o or q, some retracing is required.

retrace

ra oc rd og oq

ro

When making a horizontal join to 'o', reach all the way to the starting point of 'o' before retracing.

Trace and copy.

wa wo va vo wa vo

walk wonder vole crouch

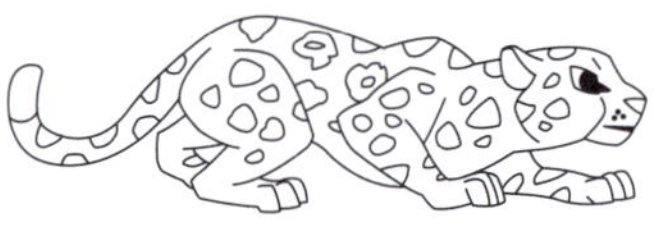

ISBN: 9780170424059

Trace and copy.

oa oc od og oo

zoo coal codfish octopus dog

ra rc rd rg ro

herd force crawl van

Give each word below an antonym, or word of opposite meaning, from the word bank. Use any joins you already know.

backwards –

broad –

wavy –

awkward –

cool –

narrow
warm
straight
graceful
forwards

ISBN: 9780170424059

Horizontal joins to head and body letters

When making a horizontal join to a head and body letter, sweep up and down, retracing a little.

Practise these letter pairs with horizontal joins to head and body letters. Trace and copy.

bb bl bt ob ok ol

ot oh rb rk rl rt

rh vl wb wk wl wh

whale rhinoceros warthog

hollow growl tortoise

Trace and copy.

Thirteen rhinos came to the

waterhole where they felt safe.

Fourteen warthogs joined their

party. Fortunately, they heard

the growl of a nearby lion

and escaped. They were okay.

Reread the text. How many animals in total at the waterhole?

ISBN: 9780170424059

Practising horizontal joins to 'e'

lower dip

be oe re ve we

Dip the join a bit lower when joining from b, o, r, v and w to 'e'.

Copy these words and sentences.

web even live rear

there covered prey tree

Spiders spin sticky webs.

They carefully wrap their

prey in delicate threads.

get.ga/PMWA163

Practising horizontal joins to 's'

When joining horizontally to 's', slide to the top of the letter 's' then retrace a little.

Trace and copy these letter pairs.

bs os rs vs ws

Copy these words.

first flippers jaws close

flutters blows grows nostril

moose osprey lobster jaws

ISBN: 9780170424059

Horizontal joins from 'f'

Trace and copy.

fe fe fe fe feed feet fear

ISBN: 9780170424059

Horizontal joins to 'f'

Continue the exit of the letter before and form a loop. Use the crossbar to join to the next letter.

Trace and copy.

of rf wf of rf wf

rfe rfu rfl rfe rfu rfl

powerful perfect overflow

Remember: when 'f' is at the beginning of a word, it doesn't need a loop.

Copy these words.

fork flight frog few fly

ISBN: 9780170424059

Double-letter pairs with horizontal joins

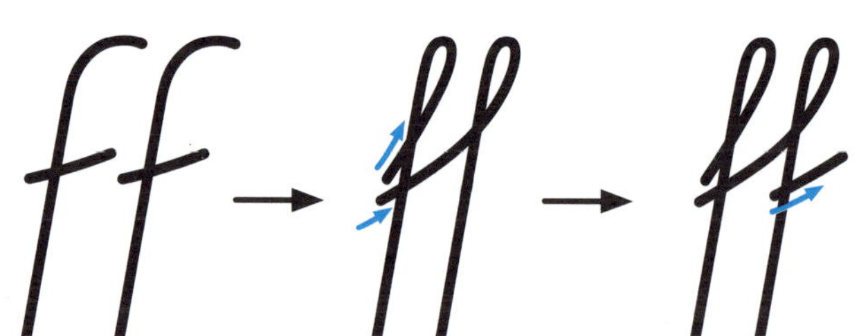

Extend the crossbar of the first 'f' upwards to make a loop for the second 'f'.

Trace and copy.

Copy these words.

different buffalo offer bluff

oss

When double 's' comes after a horizontal join, modify the shape of the second 's'.

Copy these words.

ISBN: 9780170424059

Self-assessment: Horizontal joins

Copy the text.

A large herd of caribou were

moving from the frozen north.

They sought shelter in the

mossy forests. Together, they

kept their young warm.

Self-assessment

Rate your horizontal joins.

I need more practice.

They're getting there.

They're great!

get.ga/PMWA164

ISBN: 9780170424059

Clockwise finishers

Other than 's', letters that finish in a clockwise direction do not join to the next letter.

Trace and copy these clockwise-finishing letters.

g j y z g j y z

Complete the sentence with the correct word. Then copy the sentence.

excits tails

Letters that do not join to the next letter have no ________.

Copy these words.

eight zoologist graze

dangerous glistening just

sizes lizard buzzing go

zebra amazing blaze dizzy

Put a dot between letters that will not join in cursive.

kayak grazing

jumping largest

Prove your answers by writing all four words in cursive.

ISBN: 9780170424059

Capital letters

Remember: capital letters don't join to other letters.

Trace the animal names and then write the country they live in, using cursive.

Australia Greenland India
Brazil South Africa China

reindeer ______

tiger ______

boa constrictor ______

meerkat ______

wombat ______

panda ______

ISBN: 9780170424059

Self-assessment: Letters that do not join

Rewrite the following text in cursive with capital letters in the correct places.

there are many amazing wild animals on our planet. sadly, humans don't always treat animals well. the good news is that we can help save them.

Self-assessment

How well do you remember your letters that do not join?

☐ I need more practice.

☐ I'm getting there.

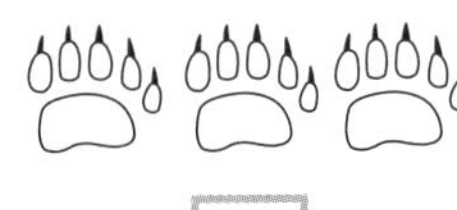

☐ I always remember!

ISBN: 9780170424059

Slope

Keeping a consistent slope makes your handwriting easier to read.

elephants ✗ elephants ✓

Practise keeping a consistent slope. Copy these words.

The giant panda is native
to China. Unfortunately,
habitat destruction has led to
the panda being endangered.

ISBN: 9780170424059

Spacing

Even spacing between letters and words helps to keep your handwriting easy to read.

Rewrite each line of text with even spacing between letters and words.

Kingfishers live all over

the world. They have big

heads, long beaks and short

legs. The most well-known

kingfisher in Australia is

the kookaburra.

ISBN: 9780170424059

Size

Rewrite the passage below, making sure your letters are the correct size.

Tigers are the largest member of the cat family. In the wild they usually live alone, but a group of tigers is known as an ambush. Tigers are most active at night.

Self-assessment: Slope, spacing and size

Copy the text, paying attention to the slope, spacing and size of your letters and words.

A rainforest is a place of

warmth and high rainfall.

It provides a safe home for

many living things, such as

monkeys, frogs and birds.

Self-assessment

How legible, or easy to read, is your handwriting?

	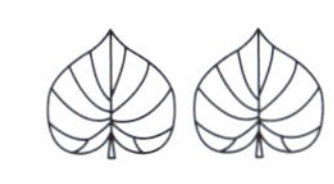	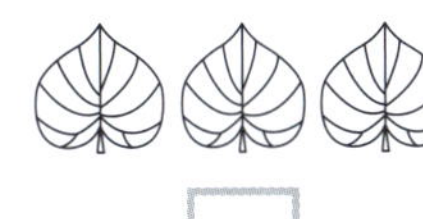
☐	☐	☐
I need more practice.	Quite legible.	Very legible!

get.ga/PMWA165

Practising all joins

Copy the text and the jokes to practise all joins. Pay close attention to writing your punctuation marks with accuracy.

Hyenas are wild animals

that like to laugh.

I hope these jokes make you laugh.

Q: What is black, white

and red all over?

A: A sunburnt penguin!

Q: Why do brown bears have fur coats?

A: Because they would look silly wearing a jacket!

Reviewing all scripts

Copy the alphabets.

a b c d e f g h i j k l m n

o p q r s t u v w x y z

abcdefghijklmnopqrstuvwxyz

A B C D E F G H I J K L

M N O P Q R S T U V W

X Y Z

Labelling diagrams

You can use unjoined letters to label diagrams.

Label the parts of the spider.

mouth legs eyes
abdomen spinneret

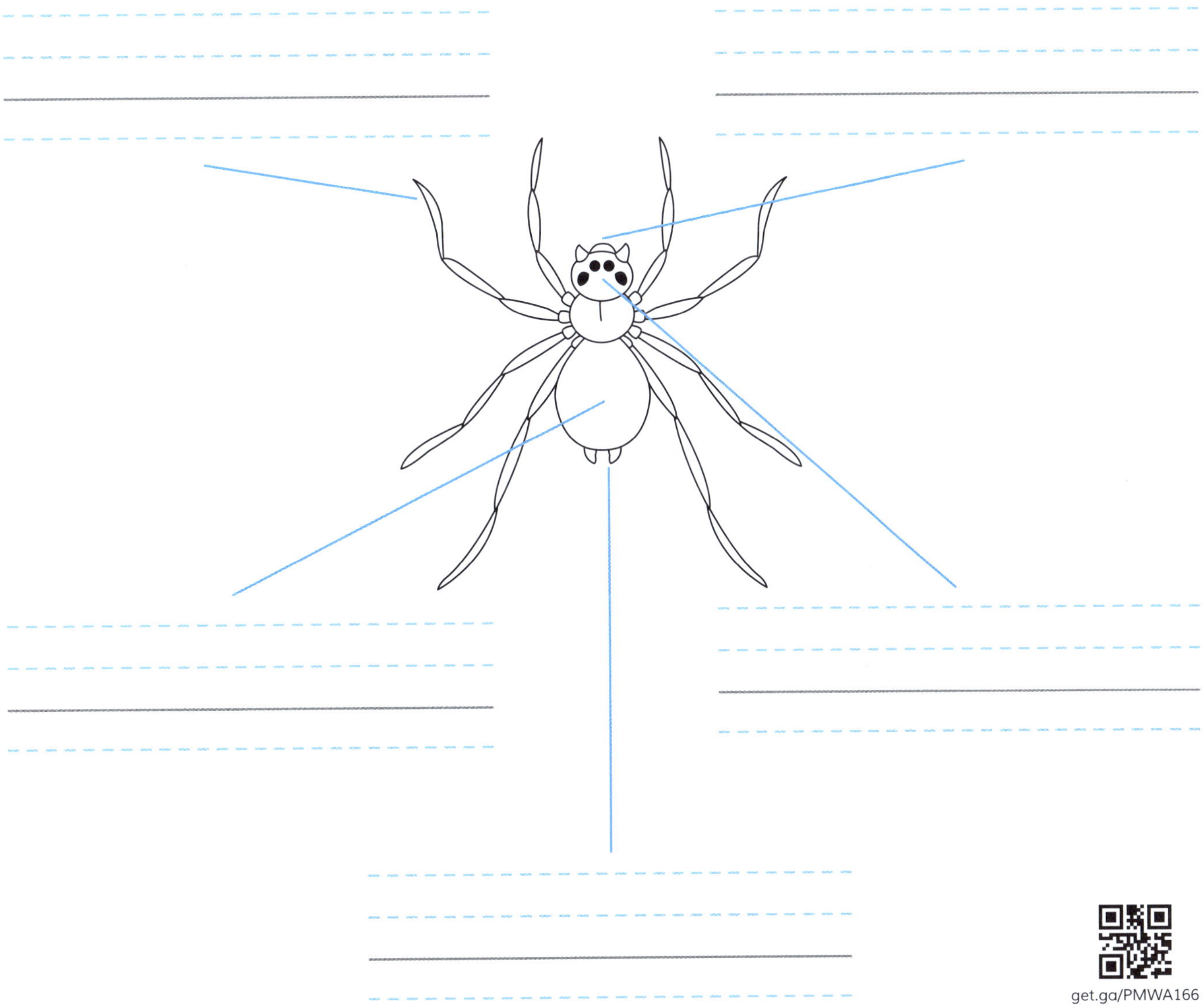

ISBN: 9780170424059

get.ga/PMWA166

Numerals

Practise your times tables. Copy and complete.

$5 \times 3 = 15$ $2 \times 7 = 14$

$10 \times 11 = 110$ $5 \times$ _____ $= 40$

$2 \times 6 =$ _____ $10 \times 12 =$ _____

$5 \times 5 = 25$ $2 \times$ _____ $= 18$

Copy the patterns on the wings of the butterflies. Make them symmetrical.

Create your own butterfly patterns. Can you copy each one carefully onto the matching wing?

ISBN: 9780170424059

Final self-assessment

Copy the text, then complete the self-assessment below.

Polar Bears are huge animals that live near the North Pole. They use their great sense of smell to hunt seals. Seal oil can make their fur yellow.

Self-assessment

Rate your Victorian Modern Cursive script.

☐ It's getting there.

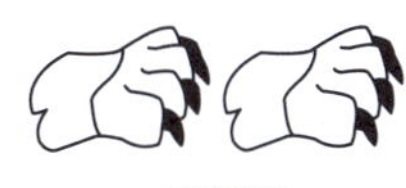

☐ Good.

☐ Excellent!

Teacher observation guide

Student is: left-handed ☐ right-handed ☐

Student demonstrates correct posture, paper position and pencil grip. ☐

Student forms the Victorian Modern Cursive alphabet (lower-case and capital letters) with accuracy. ☐

Student uses head, body and tail character to describe the spatial properties of letters, and can group letters accordingly. ☐

Student understands the four basic movement groups to which letters belong (downstroke, open anti-clockwise, closed anti-clockwise, clockwise). ☐

Student can trace and copy patterns using all three movements with accuracy. ☐

Student can identify and colour wedges. ☐

Student can identify exits and entries. ☐

Student forms diagonal joins with accuracy. ☐

Student forms touch joins with accuracy. ☐

Student forms horizontal joins with accuracy. ☐

Student can join to and from the letters 's' and 'f' with accuracy. ☐

Student can join from the letter 'q' with accuracy. ☐

Student can identify the letters that do not join in the Victorian Modern Cursive script. ☐

Student can convert between scripts: unjoined, cursive and capital letters. ☐

Student can copy a complete passage of text with accuracy in the Victorian Modern Cursive script. ☐

Student has an understanding of factors that influence legibility (slope, spacing, size). ☐

Student can self-assess with accuracy. ☐

Notes:

....

....

Date:

....

CERTIFICATE

get.ga/PMWC160